deliberate
Kindness Project

A gentle invitation to explore the impact of deliberate acts of kindness on the way you view your Self.

by

Nanci Reed

www.inomniaparatuspublishing.com

this journal was inspired by my own experience with using kindness as a way to change everything about my life. in the pages you will read about my story and i hope it inspires you to explore how you too can invite deliberate kindness and curiosity into each decision; making space to manifest your biggest dreams from the seeds of intention you've deliberately planted in all of your life.

Nanci Reed

Hi, I am Nanci Reed, welcome to my Deliberate Kindness Project - 32 Favors! This reflection journal is meant to act as both your guide and a way for you to document the impact this project has on you and the community around you.

My professional journey leading up to the initiation of the "32 Favors" project is a tapestry woven with the threads of self-discovery mixed with practical spirituality, gently blended with a lifelong passion and curiosity for guiding others toward personal growth.

I originally received an undergraduate degree in managerial economics. A few years later I received a graduate degree in Organizational Psychology with an emphasis in Emotional Intelligence and Conflict Resolution.

A pivotal near-death experience between degrees inspired me to approach my own PTSD healing via inspired journaling. Through a series of profound events I connected with my spiritual mentor and the original Teacher of 'A Course In Miracles', Dr. Kenneth (Ken) Wapnick. Through Ken's guidance I followed a lifelong curiosity surrounding the untapped power of practicing deliberate kindness.

In support of the physical healing required from my NDE, I embarked on a career as a Certified Pilates-based 'Movement Medicine ' instructor and Spiritual Life Coach.

Working in my own studios, I've been privileged to witness remarkable moments, such as clients transitioning from relying on crutches to confidently walking. My philosophy has always been about encouraging others to find their "balanced place" – a sentiment I consistently share with my clients.

The decision to launch the "32 Favors" project wasn't a spur-of-the-moment choice; it was a pivotal shift in perspective triggered by a profound dream.

Inspired by Gandhi's wisdom to "Be the change you want to see in the world," I changed my Facebook status to declare, "Nanci deserves better!" This declaration became a powerful motivator for my own journey toward a "better" life and sowed the seeds for the altruistic venture that followed.

Venturing into the blogosphere, I opened up about dreams, fears, and a particularly impactful dream that unveiled my potential to alleviate others' pain.

This realization birthed the unique concept of offering one favor per day for 32 days – a challenge that reflects not only my commitment to personal development but also a deep-seated desire to contribute positively to the global community.

Choosing to leverage my most abundant asset, time, for the collective betterment of humanity showcases my unwavering dedication to making a positive impact. The 32-day experience challenges individuals to gently overcome the perceived weakness of asking for help, creating a ripple effect of goodwill.

My journey from Pilates instructor to the architect of "32 Favors" is a testament to my commitment to continuous personal development and community well-being. The project not only mirrors my evolution as an individual but also stands as an invitation for others to embrace change, seek balance, and contribute to a world where deliberate kindness knows no bounds.

Since then I have written an award winning book, built a life of balance with the support of my family, found and teach sustainable happiness and so much more. Deliberate kindness opened the door for me to discover quantum manifestation and I am excited to help you do the same!

Imagine a life where your dreams manifest effortlessly, and perfectly imperfect sustainable happiness becomes your constant companion.

My journey, deeply influenced by 'A Course in Miracles,' unveiled this secret.

And it all started with 32 favors and deliberate kindness.

The "32 Favors" project unfolded as a poignant exploration of joy, connection, and self-discovery, with each favor revealing a unique chapter in this unexpected adventure and I knew I needed to share it,

The journey commenced with a tender request from my grandmother that set the tone for the entire project. She asked for a simple yet profound favor – to share a photo capturing a moment of pure happiness in Hawaii.

The chosen photo captured one of the happiest days of my life. In the lottery of hotel guests, I was selected to have a unique dolphin experience. This experience allowed me to swim with and hold a baby dolphin named Malia.

Be Kind & Curious

YOU KNOW WHAT LIES BEHIND YOU; THE ONLY WAY TO SEE BEYOND YOUR PAST DEFINING YOUR FUTURE IS TO FULLY EMBRACE WHAT'S IN FRONT OF YOU RIGHT NOW.

Overcoming my initial hesitations about the water, I dove in, guided by the facilitators who taught us to engage with Malia in remarkable ways, from having her jump up to grab floating rings to cradling her in my arms on the edge of the lagoon.

It was a transformative encounter, and the joy captured in that photograph echoed a profound truth – our deepest connections often happen when we allow ourselves to be the most free.

The favor that started it all...

This initial favor became more than just a photograph; it became a metaphor for the entire project.

It symbolized the liberation found in letting go of fears, embracing the unknown, and discovering profound moments of connection.

The ripple effect of that first favor set the stage for a series of favors that unfolded as interconnected stories, each offering a unique perspective on the human experience.

As the journey progressed, the favors delved into themes of forgiveness, facing fear, and starting anew. While I extended kindness to others, the project, in turn, gifted me with invaluable insights and personal growth.

The spirit of the first favor, characterized by joy and freedom, reverberated through the entire project, revealing that the true essence of connection lies in moments of uninhibited authenticity.

In the final reflection, I recognized the beauty of not needing to know the end of a story, but rather, savoring the creative process. The people encountered along the way expanded my world, proving that goodness exists even in the midst of life's challenges.

"32 Favors" was not just a blog; it was a transformative odyssey. It taught me the art of letting go, embracing the present, and approaching life with an open heart. As the project concluded, the spirit of "32 Favors" lingered, promising that the journey of understanding and kindness continues, even beyond the 32nd favor.

Lets Get Started!

setting the intention of daily kindness

what is deliberate kindness?

Deliberate kindness is a conscious, intentional act of kindness where the action is chosen with mindfulness and purpose, rather than being a spontaneous or random act.

It involves a deeper level of engagement with the world around us, guided by a clear intention to positively impact another's life or show direct kindness to ourselves. This mindfulness component is key—it means being fully present in the moment, with an acute awareness of our actions and their potential ripple effects.

Random acts of kindness are beautiful in their spontaneity and can brighten days unexpectedly. However, deliberate kindness goes a step further by embedding intentionality into the equation. It's about making a conscious decision to be kind, which can amplify the impact of the gesture, both for the giver and the receiver.

This form of kindness is rooted in a mindful approach to living, where each action is considered and aligned with the broader goal of spreading compassion and understanding.

The importance of mindfulness in deliberate kindness cannot be overstressed. It ensures that our actions are not just reactive but are a part of a thoughtful approach to life.

Mindfulness helps us recognize the needs of others as well as ourselves, guiding us to act in ways that are genuinely helpful and uplifting.

It transforms kindness from a mere act to a way of being, influencing our interactions and relationships in deeply meaningful ways.

By practicing deliberate kindness, we choose to cultivate a mindset of compassion and empathy, extending beyond random acts to a consistent pattern of behavior.

This approach fosters a sense of connection and community, creating a nurturing environment where kindness becomes a foundational element of our daily lives. Through deliberate kindness, we not only remember but actively choose to be architects of a more compassionate world, one mindful act at a time.

While building on the foundation of deliberate kindness towards others, it's essential to turn that same level of intention and mindfulness inward, embracing deliberate kindness towards ourselves.

This inward focus is not about indulgence but about recognizing our own needs and deservedness with the same compassion we extend to others. To recognize our own "Self Net Worth" even if things are not perfect. In fact, recognizing that things being "perfectly imperfect" is exactly as they should be.

Deliberate kindness to ourselves involves pausing to listen to our inner voice, acknowledging our feelings without judgment, and offering ourselves the understanding and compassion we'd extend to a dear friend.

It's about breaking the cycle of self-criticism and nurturing a supportive inner dialogue. This approach empowers us to meet our challenges with resilience.

It allows us to embrace our imperfections with grace, understanding that our worth is inherent and not contingent on external achievements or validation.

Mindfulness teaches us to be present with our experiences without getting lost in them. We learn to observe our thoughts and emotions without becoming entangled, allowing us to respond to ourselves with compassion and patience rather than harsh judgment or impatience.

This mindful approach to self-kindness lays the groundwork for a deeper connection with ourselves, fostering self-acceptance and encouraging a more authentic expression of our being.

As we embark on this journey of deliberate kindness towards ourselves, we open the door to a transformative experience. It allows us to create a nurturing inner sanctuary from which we can approach life with a grounded sense of peace and contentment.

This self-compassion not only enhances our relationship with ourselves but also deepens our capacity for kindness towards others, creating a ripple effect of positivity in our lives and the world around us.

As you move through this journal, you will find prompts that include deliberate kindness in all forms, to ourselves, to others, to our communities, stewardship on behalf of others. There are not rules around what is best. The only rule is to simply be intentionally, mindfully and deliberately kind and watch as the world around you changes.

a few gentle reminders as we get started.

Just as mindfulness is important, as you embark on this journey of self-discovery and healing, remember to give yourself the gift of space for Personal Reflection.

This isn't just about carving out time in your day; it's about creating a sanctuary within yourself for deep introspection and connection. It is about connecting your innermost being so that you are free to explore, without rush or judgment, the landscapes of your soul.

Embrace an expansive mindset that welcomes every thought, feeling, and insight with open arm while you approach everything with curiosity.

Alongside carefully crafted prompts, you are invited to dive deeply into the waters of your consciousness, exploring the contours of your dreams, fears, and desires.

This journey is yours alone, and it unfolds at a pace that feels right to you. There's no need to hurry through your reflections or force clarity; like the gentle unfolding of a flower, your insights and breakthroughs will emerge in their own perfect timing.

Remember, there's no wrong way to engage in this process of self-reflection. Whether you spend moments in quiet meditation or fill pages with your thoughts and feelings, each step is a movement towards understanding and loving yourself more fully.

One final thought before you begin officially. As you cater the experience to your own life, remember that embracing deliberate kindness as a daily practice is a big pieces of what opens the door to transformative journey.

It becomes even more powerful as you intertwine mindfulness and self reflection with your acts of kindness. The daily practice of this and mindfulness as a whole will greatly change the way you approach everything from celebrations to challenges.

Think of deliberate kindness not just as an action but as a state of being —a way to live mindfully and with intention. Each act of kindness becomes a mirror reflecting the compassion and love you harbor within.

It reinforces a cycle of positive energy that nourishes both giver and receiver. This cycle is the essence of a holistic approach to self-care and personal development, where kindness becomes the language through which you communicate with the world and yourself.

Mindfulness, the practice of being present and fully engaged with the here and now, is the foundation upon which deliberate kindness builds. It allows you to recognize opportunities for kindness in everyday moments, whether it's a smile shared with a stranger or a thoughtful gesture for a friend. Mindfulness tunes you into the subtleties of your emotions and thoughts, creating a space where self-reflection thrives.

This journey is not about grand gestures or monumental acts; it's about the small, consistent practices that shape our lives. Making deliberate kindness a daily practice means embracing every opportunity to spread joy and understanding, knowing that each act of kindness sends ripples through the fabric of the universe, touching lives in ways seen and unseen.

As you incorporate deliberate kindness, mindfulness, and self-reflection into your daily routine, remember that the goal is not to reach a destination but to savor the journey. This path leads to a deeper understanding of yourself and your place in the world, fostering a life lived with purpose, compassion, and an open heart.

Your transformation through deliberate kindness is a beautiful process that unfolds day by day. It's a journey that promises not only to change the lives of those around you but to illuminate the depths of your own soul, guiding you towards a life of abundant well-being and joy.

Welcome to your journey.

setting the intention of daily kindness

Setting the intention from the outset of this journey can truly impact your transformation. I highly recommend you start with the curiosity meditation in the tool box as well as completing the intention setting prompts.

the intention setting prompts

What drew you to the idea of having and creating a daily kindness practice?

What are you most looking forward to?

What does "Deliberate Kindness" mean to you and how is it different from Random Acts of Kindness?

What do you hope to receive from this project?

_____

_____

_____

_____

_____

_____

_____

_____

_____

_____

_____

_____

_____

_____

_____

_____

_____

_____

_____

_____

_____

_____

_____

_____

_____

_____

_____

_____

_____

_____

_____

_____

_____

_____

_____

_____

_____

_____

_____

_____

_____

_____

_____

_____

_____

_____

_____

_____

_____

_____

_____

_____

_____

_____

_____

_____

_____

_____

_____

_____

_____

_____

_____

_____

_____

_____

_____

_____

_____

_____

_____

_____

_____

_____

_____

the recipe box

a glossary

This glossary is designed to not only define key terms but also to inspire and evoke a deeper sense of connection with the concepts central to the "32 Favors" journey.

Sparkle: The radiant light that emanates from embracing one's true essence and living authentically.

Sparkle is the visible, heart-centered joy that shines through when we connect with our deepest passions, share our gifts with the world, and engage in acts of deliberate kindness.

It's not just a whimsical glimmer but rather a powerful beam, illuminating the path not only for ourselves but for others, inviting all to dance in the infinite possibilities of its gentle glow.

Sparkle Sister: A term of endearment and connection for a fellow traveler on the path to discovering and sharing their inner light. A Sparkle Sister is anyone who joins in the journey of cultivating joy, kindness, and self-discovery, lighting up the world with their unique brilliance.

a glossary

Deliberate Kindness: An intentional act of kindness, chosen with mindfulness and care, that aims to spread joy and positivity to oneself and others. It's kindness with purpose, kindness that knows where it's going and plants seeds of happiness with each step.

Heart-Centered Living: making decisions from a place of love, empathy, and deep inner connection. A heart-centered approach listens to the whispers of the heart, leading with compassion and understanding in every interaction with the world.

Gentle Agency: The power to steer your life's course with softness and grace, acknowledging that true strength lies in gentle actions and thoughtful choices. It's about embracing life's flow with intention and kindness, shaping your journey with the tender touch of a benevolent guide.

Sustainable Happiness: A deep, enduring sense of well-being that flourishes regardless of external circumstances. It's happiness that's rooted and grows from within, nourished by practices of mindfulness, gratitude, and deliberate kindness. It's the joy that lasts, blooming through all seasons of life.

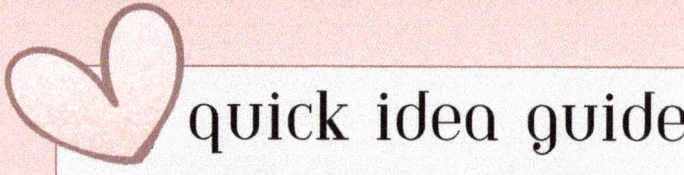

quick idea guide

A list of Free and Fast Acts of Deliberate Kindness to choose from,

1. Offer Genuine Compliments

How: Take a moment to genuinely compliment someone each day, whether it's a family member, friend, colleague, or even a stranger.

Focus on their strengths, achievements, or even their appearance in a sincere way.

2. Listen Actively

How: When someone is speaking to you, give them your full attention.

Show that you're actively listening by nodding, responding appropriately, and avoiding interruptions.

Sometimes, being heard is a profound act of kindness.

3. Leave Encouraging Notes

How: Write uplifting notes and leave them in places for others to find, such as in library books, on car windshields, or even on restroom mirrors.

Your words might offer someone the encouragement they need at just the right moment.

4. Share Knowledge or Skills

How: If you have knowledge or skills in a particular area, offer to share these with someone who could benefit.

This could be as simple as helping a neighbor with a gardening tip or tutoring a student in a subject you're proficient in.

quick idea guide

A list of Free and Fast Acts of Deliberate Kindness to choose from,

5. Express Gratitude

How: Make it a habit to express gratitude sincerely and often.

Thank someone who has helped you or made your day better, acknowledging the impact they've had on you.

6. Virtual Volunteering

How: Offer your time to virtual volunteering opportunities.

This could involve anything from graphic design for a non-profit, offering virtual tutoring, or providing support to individuals seeking advice in an area you're knowledgeable about.

7. Social Media Kindness

How: Use your social media platforms to spread kindness by posting positive messages, sharing inspirational stories, and offering supportive comments to friends and even strangers.

8. Kindness in Traffic

How: Show extra patience and courtesy while driving.

Let someone merge into your lane, or give up your parking spot for someone else.

These small acts can significantly reduce stress and spread positivity.

quick idea guide

A list of Free and Fast Acts of Deliberate Kindness to choose from,

9. Support a Friend's Project

How: Show support for a friend or family member's project or side hustle.

This can be as simple as sharing their work on social media, offering positive feedback, or just showing interest in what they're doing.

10. Smile and Greet People

How: Never underestimate the power of a smile or a friendly greeting.

Make eye contact and smile at people as you pass them on the street or greet someone warmly at the store.

These small gestures can make a big difference in someone's day.

Each of these actions embodies the essence of deliberate kindness, proving that even the smallest gesture can have a significant impact.

By incorporating these practices into your daily routine, you contribute to a ripple effect of positivity and compassion in the world.

kindness recipe

"If constantly chasing perfection has led you to waiting endlessly for the "after" in life, then embracing all of the perfect imperfection that is your life is the secret to creating your Happily Ever Now.

That may sound too simple, and hard to believe, but I'm certain that if I can do it, you can do it, too.

I'm here to show you principles that I've lived through, and that I've seen create amazing transformations in my friends' and clients' lives.

So what does "perfect imperfection" look like, you might wonder?

And what does it mean to embrace it?

Let's approach it like a recipe.

Begin with two parts deliberate kindness, mixed with one part intentional curiosity.

Next, throw in three pinches of purposeful possibility. (Make sure to fish out any sneaky shells of preconceived judgment that might have dropped into your bowl.)

Lastly, mix by hand, kneading out any lumps, and then pour into a form of your choice. Bake at 360 degrees for maximal 22 transformation, and let cool as long as needed before savoring your delicious creation.

Keep in mind that I said "pour into a form of your choice."

That was deliberate!

You get to choose how to shape your experience. The "recipe" of tools and questions in this book is meant to help you create a Happily Ever Now that is unique to you.

And it's available to you now, not after you check-off all the other "must do" boxes that someone other than you has defined as required, no matter what your Inner Perfectionist might say.

You get to choose the form, and you get to choose the instant that you're ready to begin your transformation.

pantry list

You can always choose from your own list of ingredients for your kindness recipe but here are a few ideas,

compassion

connectivity

curiosity

wonder

discovery

timeless

expansion

extension

acceptance

patience

generosity

leadership

reflection

inspiration

purpose

your recipe

We all have an ideal recipe for our deliberate kindness practice. Write yours out below.

_____

_____

_____

_____

_____

_____

the deliberate kindness adventure board

Choose 8 prompts from any of the 4 themes to complete for 8 days. I encourage you to pick at least 1 prompt from each section.

These don't need to be completed 8 days in a row and you may choose to do the same prompt or reflect on a single prompt for multiple days,

Do as many sets of 8 as you are inspired to do and feel free to create your own "favors" and acts of kindness!

There are no rules, only intention. If you complete all 32 favors, submit your game boards at the QR code below for a special gift!

the deliberate kindness adventure board

Round 1

prompt 1

prompt 2

prompt 3

prompt 4

the deliberate kindness adventure board

prompt 8

prompt 7

prompt 6

prompt 5

the deliberate kindness adventure board

Round 2

prompt 1

prompt 2

prompt 3

prompt 4

the deliberate kindness adventure board

prompt 8

prompt 7

prompt 6

prompt 5

the deliberate kindness adventure board

Round 3

prompt 1

prompt 2

prompt 3

prompt 4

the deliberate kindness adventure board

prompt 8

prompt 7

prompt 6

prompt 5

the deliberate kindness adventure board

Round 4

prompt 1

prompt 2

prompt 3

prompt 4

the deliberate kindness adventure board

prompt 8

prompt 7

prompt 6

prompt 5

join the
community

For more FREE trainings and resources, use the QR Code below to Join Sparkle Circle!

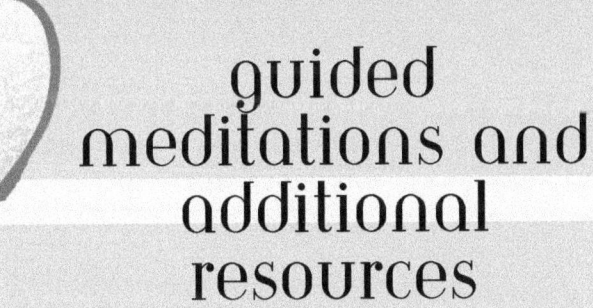

guided meditations and additional resources

At the QR code below you will find guided meditations videos that explain the prompts in more detail, additional insights into my own story and additional resources that I have crafted specifically to aid you in the completion of this journal.

In addition to the resources, there are ways to connect with me both on and off social media. I would love to hear about your journey in any way you feel called to share it with me.

the prompts

prompts 1-8
kindness to others

prompt 1: the compliment cascade

Illuminate someone's day by sharing a genuine compliment either online or in person.

Reflect on the beautiful impact of your words.

Consider the nuances that make your compliment unique and heartwarming.

prompt 2: kindness ripple

Create a ripple of kindness by extending a thoughtful gesture to a stranger.

Observe the magical ripple effect of kindness in the world.

Notice the small details and reactions, savoring the moments your kindness creates.

prompt 3: compassion connection

Cultivate compassion within by offering a listening ear to someone.

Notice the deep and meaningful connections that bloom from understanding.

Reflect on the shared humanity and the power of empathy

prompt 4: gratitude glow

Illuminate someone's life by sending a
handwritten note expressing gratitude.

Explore the impact of your written
appreciation.

Share not just what you're grateful for but
also why it matters deeply.

prompt 5: joyful service

Experience the joy of giving by engaging in an act of service for a friend or family member.

Observe the happiness that comes from selfless acts.

Reflect on the joy both you and the recipient experience.

prompt 6: affirmation affection

Shower yourself with love by sharing a positive affirmation.

Encourage others to do the same.
Witness the transformative power of self-love.

Reflect on how affirmations shape your self-perception.

prompt 7: hands and feet of love

Choose a cause close to your heart to share deliberate kindness with, either through in-person or online actions.

Reflect on the impact of being the hands and feet of love for a cause that matters deeply to you.

prompt 8: embrace loving your self

Today, create a sacred space for self-love. Begin by writing down three qualities you genuinely adore about yourself. It could be your kindness, resilience, or creativity. Indulge in a self-love ritual that resonates with you, whether it's a warm bath, a mindful meditation, or a nature walk.

As you immerse yourself in this experience, let the love you have for yourself fill every moment. Afterward, share your reflections and the details of your self-love ritual, in your inner circle, with pride.

prompt 9-16

being your own
valentine

prompt 9: a love letter to yourself

Take a moment to express your deepest admiration by writing a heartfelt love letter to yourself.

Acknowledge your achievements, express your love, and embrace your uniqueness.

This letter is a precious gift, so seal it with self-love and keep it as a reminder of your incredible worth.

Share a snippet or a meaningful quote from your love letter with your network, inspiring other Sparkle Sisters on their self-love journey.

prompt 10: self care gift

Today, give yourself the gift of self-care.

Choose an activity that brings you pure joy,
whether it's a relaxing bath, a nature walk,
or engaging in a creative endeavor.

Treat yourself as your own Valentine and
savor each moment of bliss. Capture the
essence of your self-care experience
through a photo or a vivid description, then
share it with those closest to you.

prompt 11: affirmations of self love

Craft 3-5 powerful affirmations that celebrate your self-worth and beauty.

Speak them aloud with conviction, allowing these positive words to resonate within you.

Share your empowering affirmations, creating a ripple effect of self-love among your fellow Sparkle Sisters.

prompt 12: mirror of love

Stand before the mirror and appreciate the incredible person looking back at you. Recognize your strength, beauty, and resilience.

Take a photo capturing your reflection or simply describe the feelings evoked by this self-love exercise.

Share your reflections with your closest connections, uplifting and inspiring your fellow Sparkle Sisters.

prompt 13: nourishing your self

Prepare a delightful and nourishing meal for yourself today.
Infuse each bite with self-love and gratitude for the beautiful being you are.

Share a picture of your culinary self-love adventure online or just with those closest to you, along with the recipe or the story behind your choice.

prompt 14: dance to your own rhythm

Create a playlist filled with songs that resonate with your soul.

Allow the music to guide you as you dance freely, embracing the joy within.

Share your favorite tunes or describe your dance experience with those closest to you.

Let the rhythm of self-love be felt by your fellow Sparkle Sisters.

prompt 14: bonus

Celebrate being your own Valentine,
nurturing self-love, and embracing the
uniqueness that is you.

Sparkle Sister, let your radiant self-love
journey illuminate our circle!

prompt 15: gentle self-care ritual

Today, embrace a gentle self-care ritual that nurtures your well-being.

It could be as simple as sipping a cup of tea, taking a few deep breaths, or enjoying a moment of quiet reflection.

Approach this ritual with tenderness and self-compassion.

Notice any resistance that arises and invite gentleness.

Share the details of your self-care ritual with those around you, emphasizing the importance of treating yourself with the same kindness you extend to others.

prompt 16: mirror of compassion

Stand before the mirror and practice self-compassion.
Look into your own eyes with love and understanding.
Speak words of kindness to yourself, acknowledging your journey and growth.

If resistance arises, meet it with compassion.
Share your experience with others, highlighting the transformative power of self-compassion.

prompt 17-24
kindness shared on
every level

prompt 17: journaling journey

Engage in a journaling session focused on self-compassion.

Write down moments of triumph, challenges, and self-love.
If judgment arises, shift to a compassionate perspective.

Share a snippet of your self-compassion journal with those closest to you, inspiring others to embrace self-kindness.

prompt 18: celebrating imperfections

Celebrate your perfect imperfections today.
Embrace the uniqueness that makes you authentically you.
If self-judgment arises, replace it with a loving acknowledgment of your humanity.

Share your celebration of perfect imperfections with your community, encouraging others to do the same.

prompt 19: mindful self-reflection

Engage in mindful self-reflection today. Create a sacred space to explore your thoughts and emotions with gentleness. If any resistance surfaces, approach it with curiosity and understanding.

Share insights from your mindful self-reflection with others, fostering a community of self-compassion.

prompt 20: affirmations of self-kindness

Craft 3 affirmations centered on self-kindness.
Repeat these affirmations with a compassionate tone, nurturing a positive self-dialogue.

Share your affirmations and reflections with loved ones, spreading the uplifting energy of self-kindness.

prompt 21: compassionate creativity

Express self-compassion through a creative outlet today. Whether it's art, writing, or any form of expression, let it flow from a place of gentleness.

If self-doubt arises, transform it into an opportunity for self-compassion.

Share your creative endeavor with your fellow heart-centered connections, inspiring others to explore their compassionate creativity.

May these acts of kindness towards yourself illuminate the circle with love and understanding!

prompt 22: quantum seeds of kindness

Embrace the understanding that every deliberate act of kindness, whether to yourself or others, is a seed for your quantum manifestation.

Plant a kindness seed today, and acknowledge its potential to grow into a beautiful reality.

Share your planting experience with others in your life too.

prompt 23: reflecting self-worth

Take a moment to reflect on the worthiness of your desires.

Share an inspired act of kindness that reflects your self-worth, recognizing that your dreams are valid and valuable.

prompt 24: infinite worth affirmations

Craft affirmations that affirm your infinite self-worth.
Allow these affirmations to resonate within, sharing the essence of your self-worth journey with anyone you feel inspired connect with around you.
Witness the power of your words.

♥prompt 25-32
perfectly imperfect
sustainable happiness

prompt 25: dreams in bloom

Share an act of kindness that mirrors the essence of your biggest dream.

Understand that every gesture brings your dream closer to fruition.

Embrace the blooming journey of your dreams and share the inspiration.

prompt 26: the power of presence

Be present with yourself and others. Engage in an act of mindful kindness, recognizing the transformative power of being fully present.

Share your mindful kindness moments with your loved ones too.

prompt 27: gratitude for the journey

Express gratitude for your self-worth
journey.
Share an act of kindness inspired by the
gratitude you feel for your progress.

Recognize that gratitude is a powerful force
in quantum manifestation.

prompt 28: blessings of self-net worth

Acknowledge the blessings of your
self-net worth.

Share a kindness gesture that aligns with the
blessings you've discovered within yourself.

Invite others to recognize their blessings too.

prompt 29: embracing imperfections

Celebrate your imperfections with kindness. Share an act of kindness that stems from embracing your perfectly imperfect self.

If inspired, invite others to join in the celebration too.

prompt 30: kindness as a guiding light

Consider kindness as your guiding light.
Share an inspired act of kindness that reflects the
guidance you seek in your self-worth journey.

Illuminate the path for others with your kindness.

prompt 31: quantum ripple effect

Reflect on the ripple effect of kindness.
Share an act of kindness with the awareness that
its impact extends beyond what you can see.

Witness and appreciate the ripples of your kind
actions.

prompt 32: the eternal sparkle

Celebrate the eternal Sparkle within you.

Choose an act of kindness that represents your commitment to sharing
your Sparkle and SHINE in a meaningful way that leaves a legacy of your deliberate intention.

Recognize that your journey is a perpetual cycle of giving and receiving kindness.

growing through the
reflection of daily
kindness

growing through the reflection of daily kindness

As this journey together comes to an end, I encourage you to spend time in reflection of the entire experience. Just as you have with the daily prompts, consider the changes you have seen in your life and the lives around you and answer the following questions.

the experience reflection prompts

Reflect on the themes explored during 32 Favors. Which theme resonated with you the most, and why?

What were your three greatest takeaways from practicing deliberate kindness?

How did these takeaways shape your perspective?

Share an act of kindness that had a profound impact on you.

How did this experience contribute to your self-worth journey?

In what ways did practicing deliberate kindness enhance your relationships, both with others and yourself?

How has your perception of your own worth evolved throughout this journey? Describe any mindset shifts or breakthroughs.

What challenges did you encounter, and how did you navigate them with gentleness and compassion?

Looking forward, what is one thing you commit to continuing to practice perfectly imperfectly from this moment forward?

May this closing ceremony be a celebration of your radiant journey and the eternal sparkle within you!

_____

_____

_____

_____

_____

_____

_____

_____

_____

_____

_____

_____

_____

_____

daily reflection
journaling

_____

_____

_____

_____

_____

_____

_____

_____

_____

_____

_____

_____

_____

_____

_____

_____

_____

_____

_____

_____

_____

_____

_____

_____

_____

_____

_____

_____

_____

_____

_____

_____

_____

_____

_____

_____

_____

_____

_____

_____

_____

_____

_____

_____

_____

_____

_____

_____

_____

_____

_____

_____

_____

_____

_____

_____

_____

_____

_____

_____

_____

_____

_____

_____

_____

_____

_____

_____

_____

_____

_____

_____

_____

_____

_____

_____

_____

_____

_____

_____

_____

_____

_____

_____

_____

_____

_____

_____

_____

_____

_____

_____

_____

_____

_____

_____

_____

_____

_____

_____

_____

_____

_____

_____

_____

_____

_____

_____

_____

_____

_____

_____

_____

_____

_____

_____

_____

_____

_____

_____

_____

_____

_____

_____

_____

_____

_____

_____

_____

_____

_____

_____

_____

_____

_____

_____

_____

_____

_____

_____

_____

_____

_____

_____

_____

_____

_____

_____

_____

_____

_____

_____

_____

_____

_____

_____

_____

_____

www.ingramcontent.com/pod-product-compliance
Lightning Source LLC
Chambersburg PA
CBHW051149120626
46547CB00012B/1016